For a better life
Silence

A Book on Self-Empowerment

Compiled by
M. M. Walia

NEW DAWN PRESS, INC.
USA • UK • INDIA

NEW DAWN PRESS GROUP

Published by New Dawn Press Group
New Dawn Press, Inc., 244 South Randall Rd # 90, Elgin, IL 60123
e-mail: sales@newdawnpress.com

New Dawn Press, 2 Tintern Close, Slough, Berkshire, SL1-2TB, UK
e-mail: salesuk@newdawnpress.org

New Dawn Press (An Imprint of Sterling Publishers (P) Ltd)
A-59, Okhla Industrial Area, Phase-II, New Delhi-110020, India
e-mail: info@sterlingpublishers.com
www.sterlingpublishers.com

For a better life – Silence

© 2006, Sterling Publishers (P) Ltd
ISBN 1 84557 579 2

All rights are reserved. No part of this publication may be reproduced, stored in a retrieval system or transmitted, in any form or by any means, mechanical, photocopying, recording or otherwise, without prior written permission of the publisher.

PRINTED IN INDIA

To every thing
there is a season...
a time to keep silence,
and a time to speak.

— The Bible

When all is still,

when our thoughts are quietened

and our entire nervous system

is in order,

when we have nothing against any one and
our mind is calm and poised,

then, in the inner depth of

stillness we find something which is so
ennobling and restful that

even others feel it.

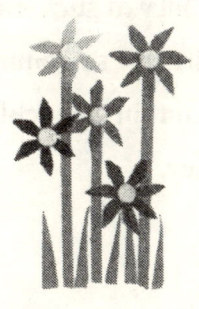

In that hour of silent co-ordination, when all our faculties are in perfect tune, we realise that we are part of the cosmic Being. It is in this ho ur that we find the fullness of our life, for then our little life has become united with the great Life, and our little mind with the cosmic Mind. Only at such moments when the finite and Infinite are so commingled, does our mind stand apart in speechless silence and unspoken wonder.

The productive life is always a silent life. When a man is creating something, he is not inclined to talk. He becomes rapt in thought and gradually, through his concentrated thoughts, he gains access to the hidden recesses of nature. He does not squander his forces by talking of each little revelation as it comes to him.

The deeper themes of life we can discover only when our mind is not disturbed by worldly agitations. Even a scientist, a musician, an artist, must have communion with his ideal, and this cannot be done without silence.

It is in the moment of silence
that we hear the voice of the Infinite.
When our ears are listening
to the loud voices of the world,
we cannot hear
the other voice
speaking in our heart.

What sleep does for our body and nervous system, silence does for our mind and spirit. The practice of silence is a very great help for acquiring evenness of mind and tranquility of body. It is experienced only when the whole being has been unified and is flowing through one channel in perfect rhythm.

Silence enables us to store up a great deal of life force which we often expend unwisely in needless talking. We wear ourselves out, disturb others, and say

much which might better be left unsaid.
We dull the mind and lessen its powers
of penetration.

❖ Silence is the only language of the realised.

❖ Most misunderstandings arise out of carelessly spoken words.

❖ Uttering falsehoods, scandalising, fault finding and excessive speech have to be avoided for peace, for the individual, as well as for society.

— Sri Sathya Sai Baba

Silence, the great unseen power, the miracle of life, works upon our character in strange contrast. At times it overwhelms us with its oppressive stillness, and again it falls upon our heart as a shower of refreshing raindrops on a sultry summer day.

Often, silence acts as a tonic, invigorating and reviving our dull spirit. Then, at other times, its effect upon us is like that of a narcotic, putting our life's energies into a state of morbid sleep. All great forces of nature work in contrast.

In the modern world, silence is often considered a negative attribute of the personality. It is unfortunate that a quiet person is branded as being reserved/introverted and not socially communicative.

But, in truth, silence helps in generating pleasantness in human relationships. It has been very rightly said — "Calumnies are answered best with silence."

Taking recourse to shouting or angry outbursts is avoidable. Furthermore, the ability to be a good listener is an important attribute of an effective conversationalist.

Silence is synonymous with Peace (*Shanti*). Therefore, if peace is the ultimate objective to attain universal happiness and eternal bliss, silence is the mode to attain it.

Saints and philosophers all over the world have used the mode of silence (*maun*) to attain communion with the higher self. The ancient hermits used to make effective use of silence as part of Yoga, as quietitude helps conserving vital energy.

In the world of spiritualism, the practice of silence plays a vital part. It creates an atmosphere which enables the seeker to find access to an inner sanctuary entirely hidden from the restless and turbulent material world. Whenever we are listening to fine music, if someone speaks or makes a noise we are distracted and jarred by it, and often we lose the subtle beauty of the music. Similarly, in spiritual study, if our attention is diverted, we receive little or no benefit. That is why the idea of complete silence is so deeply connected with spiritual thought.

Even today, we find that many places of worship maintain rigid silence in order to create an atmosphere so necessary for spiritual devotion and prayer. We can never hear the language of the soul if our ears are filled with the loud noises of the world.

The aim of silence is not to free our mind from thought and assume a state of emptiness and passivity. On the contrary, silence becomes a definite factor for efficient and concentrated thought. Silence means coordination of our body, our mind, and all our faculties to such an extent that every particle moves in rhythm.

One of the most interesting phenomena that takes place in connection with the practice of silence is that the mind evolves creative genius. For instance, when a person used to intense activity and external diversion for his pastime and pleasure is suddenly left to his own inner resources, if he is not thwarted by it, his mind will undergo a peculiar reaction and he will discover his inherent reserve and originality.

Silence and patience go together. Silence has wonderful creative powers. Great men conceive an idea, but they do not go out and shout it out to the world. They think silently and work quietly until they realise their ideal.

The habit of devoting a certain time to silent relaxation will have a very definite beneficial effect upon both our physical and moral being. During the course of our daily round of duties, we find ourselves growing physically tired or mentally tense. If we can adopt an attitude of relaxation and co-ordinate our thoughts, discarding all feelings of vexation and unrest, we shall feel restored and refreshed, and work better.

There is time for work; there is time for recreation and rest; and silence is the best restorer.

Silence is considered so necessary in India that there are great sages who become *Munis*, or silent ones. Some of them take the vow of complete silence and direct all their physical and mental forces towards spiritual illumination.

Others refrain from speaking of non-essential matters. Through this they become gifted in prophecy and the power to bless others. Even the atmosphere of the place where they live is charged with a definite spiritual force.

The practice of silence, however, does not mean merely refraining from speech. It means stilling the vital energies so that there is a cessation of all activity, both inner and outer. The body must be without motion, the mind must be serene and the heart tranquil.

The practice of physical silence restores our body and the sense organs. The practice of mental silence refreshes our mind and quickens all our inner faculties. The power gained through it is tremendous. Without deliberation and balance we can accomplish nothing worthwhile, and a moment of silence before each task enables us to maintain our balance. Its physical benefit is apparent at once. If we learn to bring ourselves to a state of absolute stillness, checking all unnecessary expenditure of force, our whole body is refreshed and strengthened. This makes the mind alert and free. Even from the point of view of wordly advantage, therefore, it is wise to practice silence.

Great things are always done silently. Whenever a life is fruitful, we shall always find that it is a life of silence. If we make our endeavour more productive, we must try never to talk unnecessarily. It is a wonderful thing to have a controlled tongue. When we have established balance at this point, we shall find that the other parts of our being will become balanced and our whole life will gain new rhythm and illumination.

The state of Grace
is the speech that arises
in the heart of silence.
— *Ramana Maharishi*

His thought is quiet,
quiet are his words and deeds,
when he has obtained
freedom by true knowledge,
when he has thus become
a quiet man.
— *The Buddha*

Silence as Yoga

There are two ways to practise silence. One is through the absence of thought, the other through fullness of thought. The second is a productive means of great strength. When we try to empty the mind, there is danger of its falling into a dull negative state, which opens it to many possible weakening influences. This is often the origin of mental depression, melancholia and those forms of insanity which are due to obsession.

When, on the contrary, we are able to fill the mind with one dynamic thought, not only does it fortify us against outer and inner dangers, but also of itself, it will empty the mind of all alien thoughts.

Even a weak person, by following this method, will soon develop a certain tranquility and strength.

Positive silence and negative silence may seem to resemble each other outwardly. Negative silence, overpowered by dullness, may appear tranquil; but it is a very different condition from the serene stillness of *positive silence*, where all the faculties of the mind are wide awake and full of light.

This higher form of silence, however, cannot be acquired in a moment. To cultivate it, we must master all our forces; and this means steady practice. First, we must try so far as we can to have a healthy body, for any physical disturbance easily destroys the silence of the mind. But a healthy body is not all; a healthy mind is better and when we have spiritual health, that is the best form of health. Since it is a less tangible form of health, people do not attach so much importance to it.

The idea of silence is not merely avoiding action; it is bringing all our scattered and undisciplined forces wholly under our control. So long as our heart is agitated, our mind stormy and our nerves distracted, it is not possible for us to have an unobstructed vision or the power of clear decision. But when the moments of stillness come, we have flashes of understanding which makes our path clear.

It is interesting to note how the practice of silence enters into the heart of every vital religion. Whether it takes the form of quiet reflection, inaudible prayer or some other special ritual of worship, it has always one aim in view, and that is to make the heart of the worshipper detached from the influences of the loud and distracting material world.

The practice of silence has to do with every part of our system. There is a silence of the body, a silence of the mind and a silence of the heart. Until all those are tranquillised, we cannot know what true silence is. The body is silent when it is free from both motion and tension. It must be wholly released, yet firm and quiet. This is gained by the practice of posture, which is one of the most essential exercises in developing the power of meditation. Posture teaches us not only to hold the body still in some fixed position at special times, but at all times to avoid every superfluous motion and maintain equilibrium. Nothing helps more to conserve our physical energies than this form of silence. It also has great healing powers.

The mind acquires silence through the persistent practice of discriminative elimination and concentration. As it comes in contact with the external world, it learns to distinguish between vital and non-vital, real and unreal; then, discarding the unreal and non-vital, it focuses itself with ardour upon the object of its attention. The heart grows still and full of gladness through meditation, which is an unbroken flow of thought and feeling towards the ideal. Only in this state do we see the manifestation of the highest intelligence.

— *Swami Parmananda*

Speak less. Work more.
Let your results speak for you.
— Pappaji (Swaminarayan Mission)

Pythagoras said that —
either it was requisite
to be silent, or to say
something better than silence.
— Stobaens

Silence is good for the wise;
how much more so for the foolish.
— *Ancient Jewish Proverb*

Experiencing Silence

Silence is a precious commodity, particularly in the hustle and bustle of modern society. In a world gone more than slightly mad, finding your core of silence is like recapturing the fort of sanity and peace. The mind replenishes itself in silence, the quantum source for all activity. If your life is dominated solely by activity, you are spending more energy than you are gaining.

Silence is a great teacher, and to learn its lessons you must pay attention to it. The great Sufi poet Rumi wrote, "Only let the moving waters calm down, and the sun and moon will be reflected on the surface of your Being."

In Communion with Nature

There is no healthier way to discharge pent-up energies than to spend time in communion with nature. In city environments it is not always easy to find a green, open space, an expansive view of the sky and clouds, a lungful of pure air.

If you can find a patch of ground to lie down on, with your shoes off and arms outstretched to the sun, take advantage of it. Short of that, seek out experiences of

Nature where you live, getting up early to appreciate the sunrise or stopping for a few moments in the evening to watch the sunset and gaze at the moon and the stars.

In order to remain centred and calm when everything around you is in confusion, you need to develop skills for finding your centre. To do that, isolate two times in your work day when things are most hectic and stressful for you (moments of heaviest workload are an obvious choice, as is the afternoon rush hour going home). Now plan to take five minutes to centre yourself just before these two periods, using the following technique.

First, black out some time to experience silence. Ideally, this would mean a short period of meditation (15 to 30 minutes) in the morning before you go to work, then a second period just after you get home in the evening. This is a time simply to be, and yet its very simplicity can make it the most important time of your life.

Find a place where you can be alone, one that is as quiet as possible. Sit comfortably and close your eyes. Pay attention to your breathing, focusing on the passage of air into and out of your nostrils. See the air as faint swirls coming into your nostrils and gently flowing out again. After two minutes, begin to feel your body (i.e., not the sensations inside your body or on your skin, the weight of your limbs, etc). After a minute, gently bring your attention to the centre of your chest and lightly rest it there. Within a few seconds your attention will probably be distracted by a fleeting thought or sensation. Don't resist this, but when you notice what is happening, gently return your focus to your chest. End the exercise by sitting quietly, doing nothing. Although this is a very simple technique, the discharge of negative energies it produces is often quite dramatic—you can feel a heavy burden lifting off your shoulders and sense a lightness and calm infusing your whole being. Most importantly, you will begin to experience that being centered is actually the most natural and comfortable way to be in any situation, no matter how hectic. Centring is a way to return to your self and become unmoored from the confusion around you.

Take time to be silent, to meditate, to quiet the internal dialogue. In moments of silence, realise that you are recontacting your source of pure awareness. Pay attention to your inner life so that you can be guided by intuition rather than externally impose interpretations of what is or isn't good for you.

Ageless Body, Timeless Mind
— Dr Deepak Chopra, M.D.

Even as fire without fuel becomes extinct in its own resting place, when thoughts become silent the mind becomes quiet in its own source.

The true silence of the mind overcomes good and evil actions.

When the mind is silent and motionless, freed from sloth and distraction, then one can enter into a state which is beyond the mind, the Supreme State.

— *Maitiri Upanishad, VI-34*

Swami Sivananda On Silence

Energy is wasted in idle talking and gossiping. *Mauna* (silence) conserves the energy, enabling you to work better mentally and physically. It has a marvellous soothing influence on the brain and nerves. By the practice of *Mauna*, the energy of speech is slowly transmuted or sublimated into spiritual energy.

Mauna develops will-force and the power of endurance, curbs the impulse of speech, and gives peace of mind.

Mauna helps in the observance of truth and controls anger. Emotions are controlled and irritability (anger) vanishes.

He who observes silence possesses peace, strength, and happiness. He is ever serene and calm. In silence, there is strength, wisdom, peace, poise, joy, and bliss.

'Mauna' Basic Guidelines

When you take a vow of silence, never assert from within, "I won't talk." This will produce a little heat in the brain, because the mind wants to react against you. Simply, make a determination and then remain quiet.

In the beginning, when you observe *Mauna*, you will find some difficulty. Various kinds of thoughts will arise and force you to break the silence. Concentrate all your energies on the higher self. Then the desire to speak and the desire for company will die. You will get peace.

You should feel that you would derive great benefit from observing *Mauna* and experience peace, inner strength and joy. Forced *Mauna*, simply to imitate someone or due to compulsion, will make you restless.

Discipline of Speech

Try to become a person of measured words. Strictly avoid long talk, big talk, all unnecessary talk, and withdraw yourself within your inner self as much as possible. This is real *Mauna*. To talk profusely for six months and to observe *mauna* for the rest of the year will be of no avail.

Watch every word you speak. This is the greatest discipline. Words are great forces. Use them carefully. Control your speech.

Purify the mind and reflect. Be still, and calm the mind. Silence all bubbling thoughts and surging emotions. Plunge deep into the innermost recess of your heart and enjoy the magnanimous silence. Mysterious is this silence. Enter into silence. Know that silence. Become silence itself.

Physical Silence and Silence of the Mind

To sit quiet is silence. But this is only physical silence. What is really needed is silence of the mind. You may observe the vow of silence, but the mind will be building images. Imagination, reasoning, reflection, and various other functionings of the mind will be going on continuously. There can be no real peace or silence now. The intellect should cease functioning. The inner waves of the mind should completely subside. The mind should rest in *Brahman* or the ocean of silence. Then only can you enjoy real, everlasting silence.

— *Swami Sivananda*

"If water derives lucidity from stillness,

how much more the faculties of the mind!

The mind of the sage,

being in repose,

becomes the mirror of the universe,

the speculum of all creation."

– Chuang Tzu

"Silence is as deep as eternity,

speech as shallow as time."

– Carlyle

"Be silent
that the Lord who gave thee
language may speak,
for as He fashioned a door and lock,
He has also made a key...
I am silent."
– *A Sufi Mystic*

Words of Wisdom on Silence

- Train yourself in the language of God. Silence is His language.

    – Swami Sivananda

- The more you talk, the more likely you are to sin. If you are wise, you will keep quiet.

    – The Bible

- He is not one of me, but a rebel at heart who when he speaketh, falsely: who when he promiseth, breaketh his promise: and who when trust is reposed in him, faileth in his trust.

    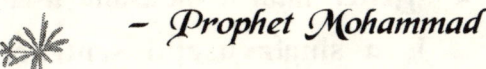 – *Prophet Mohammad*

- What necessity is there for a man to speak when he has reached the highest spiritual stage?

    – *Sant Kabir*

- Not that which goeth into the mouth defileth a man, but that which comes out of his mouth, this defileth a man.

  – The Bible

- Better than a thousand useless words, is a single useful sentence, hearing which, one is pacified.

  – The Buddha
  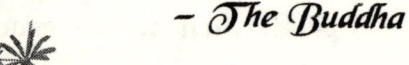

- A word spoken in wrath is the sharpest sword; covetousness is the deadliest poison; passion the fiercest fire; and ignorance the darkest night.

– The Buddha

- Every idle word that men shall speak, they shall give account thereof on the day of judgement.

– The Bible

- Do not speak ill of the departed.

– Swami Sivananda

Mahatma Gandhi on Silence

Silence is a great help to the seeker of truth. In the attitude of silence the soul finds the path in a clearer light and what is elusive and deceptive resolves itself into crystal clearness. Our life is a long and arduous quest after Truth and the soul requires inward restfulness to attain its full height.

Experience has taught me that silence is a part of the spiritual discipline of a votary of truth. Proneness to exaggerate, to suppress or modify the truth wittingly or unwittingly, is a natural weakness of man, and silence is necessary in order to surmount it. A man of few words will rarely be thoughtless in his speech; he will measure every word.

It is only in silence that true progress can be made; It is only in silence that one can rectify a wrong movement; It is only in silence that one can be of help to somebody else.

— *The Mother*

The love of solitude is a sign of disposition towards knowledge.

You must remain and grow always more and more deeply quiet and still, both in yourself and in your attitude to the world around you.

— *Sri Aurobindo*

I often wish that I had kept silent. The reason why we so willingly talk is that by discoursing together we seek comfort from one another; and we wish to ease our hearts, wearied by various thoughts.

If it be lawful and expedient to speak, speak those things which may edify.

— *Thomas A Kempis*

Saint Tayumanavar On Silence

If I am established in the pure quiescence, I shall automatically attain the silence of intellect, mind, word, and actions.

Silence is the resultant state when the I, ego, which asserts that 'I' am the only thing that ever exists, falls down abashed, and in its place the Self, the Reality, arises as the fullness.

From silence, ego arises in the form of 'I'; from the 'I' arises thought, and from thought arises words; so the spoken word is the great grandson of silence.

Renouncing everything, one may ever abide in great silence. Thus, one may free oneself from an impure mind, devoid of thought processes and intellect. By rejoicing in silence, one can be rooted in full knowledge.

Types of Silence

The ancient Hindu scriptures classify silence into four types: (i) *Vak mouna* (abstention from speech), (ii) *mano mouna* (silence — free from mental activity), (iii) *karana mouna* (keeping all external organs - like feet and hands — motionless), and (iv) *kasta mouna* (abstention from all activities of inner and outer organs, including the mind).

The best of the four is *kasta mouna*, which is total abstention from all objective and subjective movements.

Adi Sankaracharya On Silence

We have all read that the highest form of teaching is silence and that it was conveyed through silence by Lord Daksinamurti. We can easily comprehend a teaching communicated to us through the conveyance of words, but how can we understand a teaching conveyed in silence? Is it possible at all in modern times? Yes, in Sri Ramana Maharshi we saw an embodiment of silence. In his presence one experienced the immensity of the power of silence. After Lord Daksinamurti, Bhagavan Ramana alone lived and taught the glorious teaching of silence, in silence.

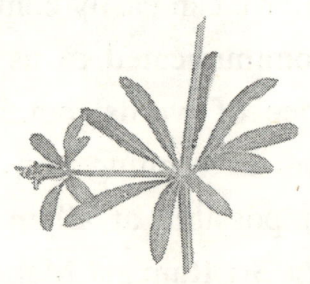

J Krishnamurti on Silence

The only silence we know is the silence when noise stops, the silence when thought stops— but that is not silence. Silence is something entirely different, like beauty, like love. And this silence is not the product of a quiet mind, it is not the product of the brain cells that have understood the whole structure and say, "For God's sake be quiet"; then the brain cells themselves produce the silence and that is not silence. Nor is silence the outcome of attention in which the observer is the observed; then there is no friction; but that is not silence.

That silence, which is not the silence of the ending of noise, is only a small beginning. It is like going through a small hole to an enormous, wide, expansive ocean, to an immeasurable, timeless state.

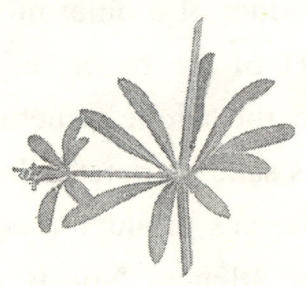

Sri Ramana Maharshi on Silence

A Guru's silence is the loudest instruction. Silence is also grace in its highest form.

Your real state is silence. One is always in that state of silence. That is disturbed by the birth of the I-thought. Only after the rise of the I-thought do other thoughts arise. When other thoughts arise, ask oneself for whom these thoughts are, and where this "I" arises from. Thus diving within, if one traces the sources of the mind and reaches the heart, one becomes the supreme Reality, the eternal state of total silence.

The silence of solitude is forced. Restrained speech in society amounts to silence, for the man then controls his speech. The speaker must come forth before he speaks. If engaged otherwise, speech is restrained. The introverted mind is otherwise active and is not anxious to speak.

Mouna (silence) as a disciplinary measure is meant for limiting the mental activities due to speech. If the mind is otherwise controlled, disciplinary *mouna* is unnecessary, for *mouna* becomes natural.

It has been said that twelve years of forced *mouna* brings about absolute *mouna* — that is, makes one unable to speak. It is more like a mute animal. That is not *mouna*.

Through the practice of silence, we gain knowledge of our spiritual nature and bring our external nature into harmony with it.

Stillness is not negative. It is not the lack of life; it is the control of life. Silent power is always constructive. The practice of silence helps us gain a glimpse of our internal nature. That is why wise men have spent so much time in silence. Unless we have the quiet of mind, unless we have learned to control our restless thoughts, we cannot be unmoved in all the experiences of life.

— *Swami Paramananda*

Being alone does not mean being lonely. It means cutting off the external, the superficial and the superfluous, and seeking instead the inner strength which one finds best in solitude. It enriches the spirit and ennobles the man, and one who denies himself its refuge is not living life to its fullest.

— *Henry King*

Silence, along with modesty, is a great aid to conversation.

— *Montaigne*

Gems of Wisdom on Silence

❖ Blessed are they who have nothing to say, and who cannot be persuaded to say.

— Lowell

❖ Silence helps one to suppress one's anger, as perhaps nothing else does.

— Mahatma Gandhi

❖ The unspoken word never does harm.

— Kossuth

❖ Even a fool, when he holdeth his peace, is counted wise.

– *The Old Testament*

❖ This is such a serious world that we should never speak at all unless we have something to say.

– *Thomas Carlyle*

❖ Be silent or let your words be worth more than silence.

– *Pythagoras*

❖ Vessels never give so great a sound as when they are empty.

— John Jewell

❖ Silence is the most perfect expression of scorn.

— George Bernard Shaw

❖ Silence is one great art of conversation.

— Hazlitt

Mother Teresa on Silence

In the silence of our hearts, God speaks and from the fullness of our hearts we speak.

See how nature, the trees, the flowers, and the grass grows in perfect silence; the stars, the moon and the sun, how they move in silence.

Silence is at the root of our union with God and with one another.

The fruit of silence is prayer.
The fruit of prayer is faith;
The fruit of faith is love; and
The fruit of love is service.

The word "mauna" means silence. The word comprises two syllables – "ma" and "na". "Ma" is "*manas*" (mind) and "na" is "*nahi*" (no). Therefore "*mauna*" means the state where there is no mind. It implies that the mind is not disturbed by emotions, thoughts, desires, feelings and so on. When you achieve "mindlessness", you can then hear the Divine voice that is the voice of *Antra-atma* or the Inner voice.

When one is able to quieten the mind, control one's thoughts and be free from any unrest and mental disturbances, then only is it possible to tune in to the inner voice.

When the mind is peaceful and quiet, one has extra energy, which is otherwise being wasted in unnecessary talk. Consequently, one will be able to think better and perform his duties more efficiently. Therefore, it is good to practice *mauna* for sometime every day and feel peace and extra energy in your daily routine.

Silence is *Soham*. Silence is the voice of God.

– *Sri Sathya Sai Baba*

Be good silently.

Do good silently.

Love God and men silently.

Do your duty silently.

Accept God's will silently.

Be happy with others silently.

Conceal another's faults silently.

Wish and aspire secretly and silently.

Embrace the Cross of Jesus silently.

Sacrifice and resign yourself silently.

Look towards Heaven silently.

Attain virtue silently.

Persevere until death silently.

– General Manueal A Rodrigues

Men seek retreats for themselves, houses in the country, seashores and mountains; and thou too art wont to desire such things very much. But it is within thy power, whenever thou shalt choose, to retire into thyself. For nowhere, either with more quiet or more freedom from trouble, does a man retire than into his own soul, particularly when he has within him such thoughts that, looking into them, he is immediately in perfect tranquillity.

Look within. Within is the fountain of good.

— *Marcus Aurelius*

In today's crowded civilization and in this busy and active society, man is finding it increasingly difficult to indulge one of the most priceless luxuries which life can give: occasional total solitude.

— *Henry King*

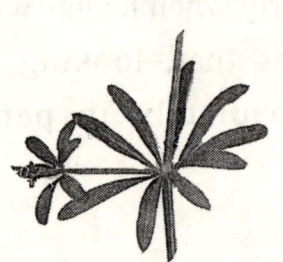

Three Kinds of Silence

- Silence from words is good, because inordinate speaking tends towards evil.
- Silence, or rest from desires and passions is still better, because it promotes quietness of spirit.
- But the best of all is silence from unnecessary and wandering thoughts, because that is essential to internal recollection; and because it lays a foundation for a proper reputation and for silence in other respects.

Gems of Wisdom

❖ One of the first principles of straight living is the practice of silence. For the voice of God can be heard in the region of your heart only when the tongue is stilled and the inner storm is subdued and the waves are calm.

❖ Be silent yourself; that will induce silence in others. Carry with you an atmosphere of quiet contemplation, wherever you happen to be. Do not fall into the habit of shouting or talking long and loud.

❖ A talkative person easily steps into scandal mongering. Too much talk and a tongue addicted to scandal are twins; they work together and in unison.

❖ The ancients practised three kinds of silent penance. One was silence of the tongue (*vaak-maunam*); the second was silence of the mind (*mano-mounam*); the third was supreme silence (*maha mounam*).

— *Sri Sathya Sai Baba*

Control of the Tongue and Speech

❖ Be very careful about your speech. Animals have horns, insects have stings, beasts have claws and fangs. But man's biggest weapon of offense is his tongue. The wounds caused by it take long to heal.

❖ The first step in *sadhana* is the cleansing of one's speech. Speak sweetly without anger. Do not boast of your scholarship or attainments. Be humble, eager to serve. Conserve your speech. Practise silence. That will save you from squabbles and from frittering away your time.

- ❖ The tongue should be used for spelling the Name of the Lord and not for hissing like a serpent or growling or roaring with the intention to infuse terror.
- ❖ The tongue is the armour of the heart; it guards one's life. Loud talk, long talk, wild talk, talk full of anger and hate, all these will affect the health. They breed anger and hate in others.

❖ The first lesson in the primer of this spiritual text is "the control of speech".

❖ The numbers of those who talk pleasantly is large because they need only cater to man's pleasure. But the number of those who talk usefully, profitably, beneficially, is small, for few know what is really useful, profitable and beneficial for man in the long run.

❖ *Vaak* (voice) has to be religiously trained to avoid chatter and senseless prattle. Keep the tongue under control; do not express all that you are prompted to say; cut that inclination to the minimum. Silence will charge the battery.

- ❖ Soft, sweet speech is the expression of genuine love. Hate screeches, fear squeals, conceit trumpets. But love sings lullabies, it soothes, it applies balm. Practice the vocabulary of love, and unlearn the language of hate and contempt.

- ❖ Speech can give insight into one's character, so be careful about the words you utter. A slip while walking can be repaired, but a slip while talking can cause irreparable injury. Words should be used only to seek and see symmetry, harmony and beauty.

— *Sri Sathya Sai Baba*